Angels Helper
Sign Language
Coloring
and
Activity Book

GLENDA SMITH

authorHOUSE

AuthorHouse™
1663 Liberty Drive
Bloomington, IN 47403
www.authorhouse.com
Phone: 1 (800) 839-8640

Published by AuthorHouse 10/29/2019

ISBN: 978-1-7283-3362-5 (sc)
ISBN: 978-1-7283-3360-1 (hc)
ISBN: 978-1-7283-3361-8 (e)

Library of Congress Control Number: 2019917278

Print information available on the last page.

This book is printed on acid-free paper.

This book is dedicated to my Great Grand Daughter
Lovely Monet Alexander with Love

CONTENTS

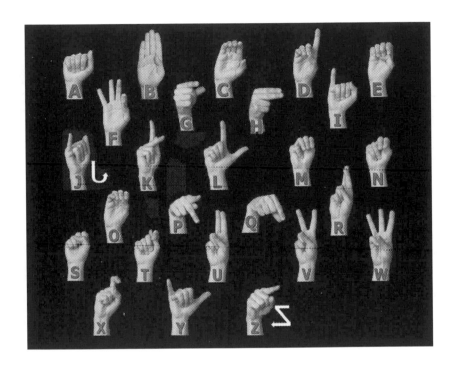

lifeprint.com

Bingo

A N G E L

A N G E L

A N G E L

ANGELS ARE HELPERS OF GOD

A-N-G-E-L, A-N-G-E-L,
A-N-G-E-L,

ANGELS are helpers of God
Los ángeles son ayudantes de Dios

A a

Angels – helpers of God

Exodus 23:20

"Behold, I am going to send an angel before you to guard you along the way and to bring you into the place which I have prepared."

Éxodo 23:20

"Mira, voy a enviar un ángel delante de ti para que te guarde en el camino y te lleve al lugar que he preparado".

B-I-B-L-E, B-I-B-L-E,
B-I-B-L-E,

The BIBLE is the Word of God

La biblia es la palabra de dios

Bible – the Word of God

Psalm 119: 105

Your word is a lamp to my feet and a light for my path.

Salmo 119: 105

Tu palabra es una lámpara para mis pies y una luz para mi camino.

2 Timothy 3:16-17

All Scripture is inspired by God and profitable for teaching, for reproof, for correction, for training in righteousness; so that the man of God may be adequate, equipped for every good work.

2 Timoteo 3: 16-17

Toda la Escritura está inspirada por Dios y es provechosa para enseñar, para redargüir, para corregir, para entrenar en justicia; para que el hombre de Dios sea adecuado, equipado para toda buena obra.

C-R-O-S-S, C-R-O-S-S, C-R-O-S-S,

THE CROSS is where Jesus died
La cruz es donde murió Jesús

Cc

Cross – where Jesus was crucified and died

1 Corinthians 1:18

For the word of the cross is foolishness to those who are perishing, but to us who are being saved it is the power of God.

1 Corintios 1:18

Porque la palabra de la cruz es necedad para los que perecen, pero para nosotros que somos salvos es el poder de Dios.

THE CROSS APPLIES TO:

D-A-V-I-D, D-A-V-I-D, D-A-V-I-D

DAVID The King appointed by GOD

David King designado por Dios

Dd

David – King appointed by God

Acts 13:22

After He had removed him, He raised up David to be their king, concerning whom He also testified and said, "I HAVE FOUND DAVID the son of Jesse, A MAN AFTER MY HEART, who will do all My will."

Hechos 13:22

Después de haberlo eliminado, levantó a David para que fuera su rey, de quien también testificó y dijo: "HE ENCONTRADO A DAVID, hijo de Jesé, UN HOMBRE DESPUÉS DE MI CORAZÓN, que hará toda mi voluntad".

KING DAViD   VS GOLIATH

MEEK

MIGHTY

THE WORLD
EARTH

JESUS CONTROLS

E-A-R-T-H, E-A-R-T-H, E-A-R-T-H,

THE EARTH BELONGS TO THE LORD

La tierra le pertenece a Dios

Earth – The Earth is the Lord's

Psalm 24:1

The earth is the Lord's, and all it contains, The world, and those who dwell in it.

Salmo 24: 1

La tierra es del Señor, y todo lo que contiene, el mundo y los que moran en ella.

F-A-I-T-H, F-A-I-T-H, F-A-I-T-H,

CAN NOT PLEASE GOD WITHOUT FAITH

No puede agradar a Dios sin fe

F f

Faith – can not please God without faith

Hebrews 11:6

And without faith it is impossible to please *Him*, for he who comes to God must believe that He is and *that* He is a rewarder of those who seek Him.

Hebreos 11: 6

Y sin fe es imposible agradarlo, porque el que viene a Dios debe creer que Él es y que es un galardonador de los que lo buscan.

G-L-O-R-Y, G-L-O-R-Y, G-L-O-R-Y

GOD'S GLORY FILLS THE EARTH
La gloria de Dios llena la tierra

GLORY-HIS GLORY FILLS THE EARTH

EXODUS 33:18
Then Moses said, "I pray you, show me your glory!"

Éxodo 33:18
Entonces Moisés dijo: "¡Te ruego, muéstrame tu gloria!"

PSALM 85:9

Surely His salvation is near to those who fear Him, that **glory** may dwell in our land.

SALMO 85: 9

Seguramente su salvación está cerca de aquellos que le temen, para que la gloria pueda habitar en nuestra tierra.

GOSPEL TO GLORY

! REJOICE!

REJOICE IN THE LORD

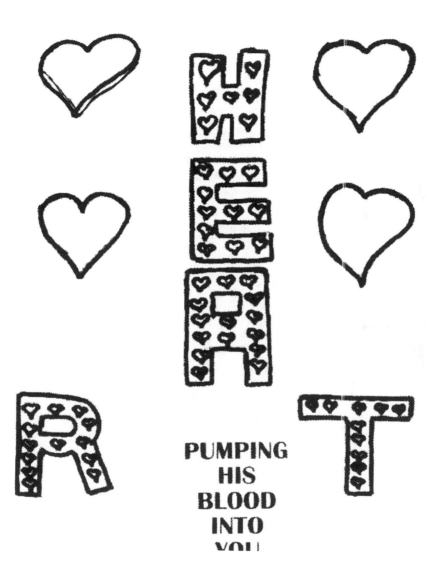

HEART PUMPING HIS BLOOD INTO YOU

IT'S A HEART TO HEART MATTER

H-E-A-R-T, H-E-A-R-T, H-E-A-R-T

GOD looks on man's HEART
Dios mira el corazón del hombre

H h

HEART-GOD LOOKS ON THE HEART OF MAN

1 SAMUEL 16:7

But the LORD said to Samuel, "Do not look at his appearance or at the height of his stature, because I have rejected him; for God *sees* not as man sees, for man looks at the outward appearance, but the LORD looks at the heart."

EZIEKIEL 36:26

Moreover, I will give you a new heart and put a new spirit within you; and I will remove the heart of stone from your flesh and give you a heart of flesh.

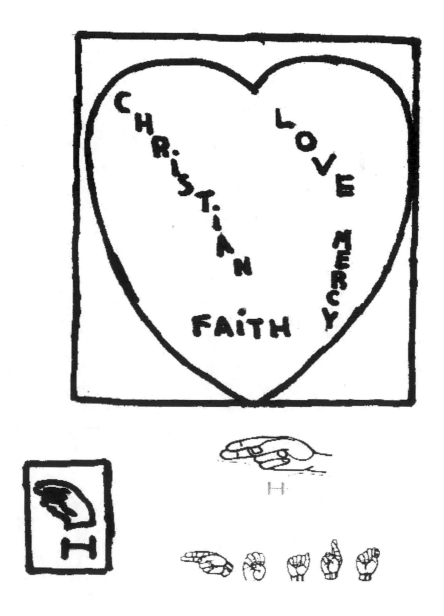

I-S-A-A-C, I-S-A-A-C, I-S-A-A-C

ISAAC was the son of Abraham

Isaac era el hijo de Abraham

I i

Genesis 18: 10

Then one of them said, "I will return to you about this time next year, and your wife, Sarah, will have a son!"

Génesis 18:10

Entonces uno de ellos dijo: "¡Volveré a hablar sobre usted en esta época el próximo año, y su esposa, Sarah, tendrá un hijo!"

ABRAHAM AND ISAAC

RESTORED THROUGH FAITH !

J-E-S-U-S, J-E-S-U-S, J-E-S-U-S,

JESUS is the son of God
Jesús es el hijo de dios

J j

Luke 2:21

And when eight days had passed, before His circumcision, His name was then called Jesus, the name given by the angel before He was conceived in the womb.

Lucas 2:21

Y cuando pasaron ocho días, antes de su circuncisión, su nombre se llamó Jesús, el nombre dado por el ángel antes de ser concebido en el útero.

LISTEN TO JESUS AND BE OBEDIENT. PRAY FOR THE FORGIVENESS OF OUR SINS!

LISTEN TO JESUS
AND BE OBEDIENT
FOR HIM FORGIVING
US FOR OUR SINS!

el Angel

K-I-N-G-S, K-I-N-G-S, K-I-N-G-S

JESUS IS KING OF KINGS

Jesús es rey de reyes

K k

1 Timothy 6: 15

Which He will bring about at the proper time—He who is the blessed and only Sovereign, the King of kings and Lord of Lords,

1 Timoteo 6:15

Lo cual traerá en el momento apropiado: el que es el bendito y único Soberano, el Rey de reyes y Señor de señores,

L-I-G-H-T, L-I-G-H-T, L-I-G-H-T

Jesus is the LIGHT of the world

Jesús es la luz del mundo

L I

John 12:36

While you have the Light, believe in the Light, so that you may become sons of Light.

JUAN 12:36

Mientras tengas la Luz, cree en la Luz, para que puedas convertirte en hijos de la Luz.

HE IS THE LIGHT OF THE WORLD

M-E-R-C-Y, M-E-R-C-Y, M-E-R-C-Y

HE Shows us Grace and MERCY
Nos muestra gracia y misericordia

M m

Psalm 145:9

The LORD is good to all, and His mercies are over all His works.

Salmo 145: 9

El SEÑOR es bueno con todos, y sus misericordias están sobre todas sus obras.

HE TOUCHED ME FROM THE TOP OF MY HEAD TO THE BOTTOM OF MY FEETEH

ME TOUCHED ME FROM MY HEAD TO MY FEET

POWER OF LOVE

N-O-I-S-E, N-O-I-S-E, N-O-I-S-E

Make a joyful NOISE unto HIM

Hazle un ruido alegre

N n

Psalm 100: 1

Make a joyful noise unto the LORD, all ye lands.

Salmo 100: 1

Haz un ruido alegre al SEÑOR, todas las tierras.

N
O
I
S
E

HEAVEN'S DOORS AND WINDOWS ARE OPEN TO US

O-P-E-N-S, O-P-E-N-S, O-P-E-N-S

He OPENS closed doors
Abre puertas cerradas

Rev 3:8

'I know your deeds. Behold, I have put before you an open door which no one can shut, because you have a little power, and have kept My word, and have not denied My name.'

Apocalipsis 3: 8

'Conozco tus obras. He aquí, he puesto ante ustedes una puerta abierta que nadie puede cerrar, porque tienen un poco de poder y han cumplido Mi palabra y no han negado Mi nombre ".

P-R-A-Y-S, P-R-A-Y-S, P-R-A-Y-S

He listens when we PRAY
Él escucha cuando rezamos

1 Thessalonians 5:17

Pray without ceasing

1 Tesalonicenses 5:17

Orar sin cesar

Q-U-I-E-T, Q-U-I-E-T, Q-U-I-E-T

Listen to His quiet spoken Word

Escuche su tranquila palabra hablada

Ecclesiates 9:17

The quiet words of the wise are more to be heeded than the shouts of a ruler of fools.

Eclesiados 9:17

Las palabras tranquilas de los sabios son más a tener en cuenta que los gritos de un gobernante de tontos.

R-I-S-E-N, R-I-S-E-N, R-I-S-E-N

He is RISEN from the dead
Ha resucitado de la muerte

R r

Matthew 28:6

He is not here; for he has risen, just as He said. Come, see the place where He was lying.

Mateo 28: 6

Él no está aquí; porque ha resucitado, tal como lo dijo. Ven, mira el lugar donde estaba acostado.

HE IS RISEN FROM THE DEAD

HE ROSE SO WE MIGHT LIVE AGAIN

S-E-R-V-E, S-E-R-V-E, S-E-R-V-E

Be willing to SERVE the Lord
Estar dispuesto a servir al Señor

S s

Galatians 5:13

For you were called to freedom, brethren; only *do* not *turn* your freedom into an opportunity for the flesh, but through love serve one another.

Gálatas 5:13

Porque ustedes fueron llamados a la libertad, hermanos; solo no conviertas tu libertad en una oportunidad para la carne, sino que a través del amor sirvanse unos a otros

T-A-B-L-E,-T-A-B-L-E, T-A-B-L-E

The Lord's TABLE is set
La mesa del Señor está puesta

T t

Psalm 23:5a
You prepare a table before me in the presence of my enemies.

Salmo 23: 5a
Preparas una mesa delante de mí en presencia de mis enemigos.

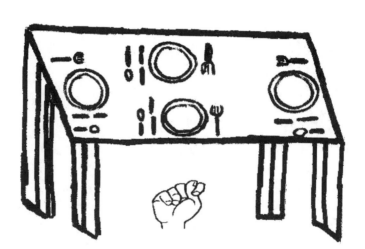

THE LORD'S TABLE iS SET

Angel

U-P-P-E-R, U-P-P-E-R, U-P-P-E-R

What a time in the UPPER room
Que tiempo en el aposento alto

U u

Acts 1:13-14

When they had entered *the city*, they went up to the upper room where they were staying; that is, Peter and John and James and Andrew, Philip and Thomas, Bartholomew and Matthew, James *the son* of Alphaeus, and Simon the Zealot, and Judas *the son* of James.

These all with one mind were continually devoting themselves to prayer, along with *the* women, and Mary the mother of Jesus, and with His brothers.

Hechos 1: 13-14

Cuando entraron en la ciudad, subieron a la habitación superior donde se alojaban; es decir, Peter y John y James y Andrew, Philip y Thomas, Bartholomew y Matthew, James, hijo de Alfeo, y Simón el Zelote, y Judas, hijo de James. Todos ellos con una sola mente se dedicaban continuamente a la oración, junto con las mujeres, y María, la madre de Jesús, y con sus hermanos.

V-E-R-S-E, V-E-R-S-E, V-E-R-S-E

Study Your Bible VERSE by VERSE

Estudia tu versículo de la biblia por verso

V v

Study to show thyself approved unto God
2 Tim 2:15

Estudia para mostrarte aprobado a Dios
2 Tim 2:15

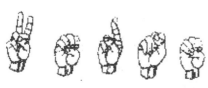

W-R-O-T-E, W-O-R-T-E, W-R-O-T-E

My name is WROTE in the Book
Mi nombre esta escrito en el libro

W w

Isaiah 30:8

Now go, write it before them in a table, and note it in a book, that it may be for the time to come for ever and ever:

Isaías 30: 8

Ahora ve, escríbelo delante de ellos en una tabla y anótalo en un libro, para que sea el momento por siempre y para siempre:

LISTEN TO GOD

RCA

AM   FM

53 70 88 92 96 100 102

THROUGH THE PREACHED WORD
TV, RADIO, ETC.

E-X-A-L-T, E-X-A-L-T, E-X-A-L-T

We EXALT THEE OH LORD
Exaltamos al Señor

X x

Psalm 34:3

O magnify the LORD with me; And let us **exalt** His name together.

Salmo 34: 3

Magnifica al SEÑOR conmigo; Y exaltemos su nombre juntos.

Y-A-H-W-E-H,
Y-A-H-W-E-H,
Y-A-H-W-E-H

YAHWEH, Hebrew name of God
Yahew nombre hebreo de Dios

Psalms 135

Praise Yahew! Praise Yahweh's name!

Salmos 135

¡Alabado sea Yahew! ¡Alabado sea el nombre de Yahweh!

Z-O-N-E, Z-O-N-E, Z-O-N-E

Our church is a GOD ZONE

Nuestra iglesia es una zona de Dios.

Z z

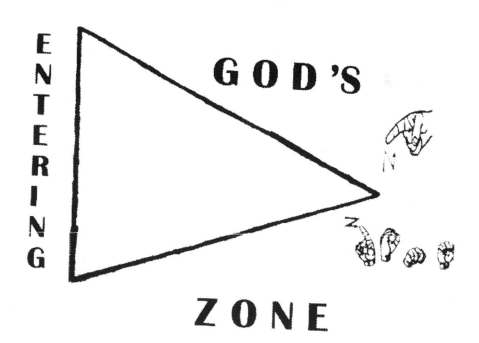

PRINCIPLES TO LIVE BY

Show Love
Be Honest
Outreach with Compassion
Community Involvement
Excellence
Help the Poor
Muestra amor
Se honesto
Alcance con compasión
Participación de la comunidad
Excelencia
Ayudar al pobre

Scripture:

"For I was hungry and you gave me something to eat; I was thirsty and you gave me something to drink; I was a stranger and you invited me in; Naked and you clothed me; I was sick and you visited me; I was in prison and you came to me." Matthew 25: 35-36 NASB

"Porque tenía hambre y me diste algo de comer; Tenía sed y me diste algo de beber; Yo era un extraño y me invitaste a entrar; Desnudo y me vestiste; Estaba enfermo y me visitaste; Estaba en prisión y tú viniste a mí ". Mateo 25: 35-36 NASB

SCRIPTURES FOR EACH LETTER OF ALPHABET

All have sinned and fallen short of the Glory of God (Romans 3:23)

Be kind one to another (Eph. 4:32)

Children obey your parents, for this is the right thing to do (Eph. 6:1)

Don't fret or worry, it only leads to harm (Psalm 37:8)

Every good and perfect gift comes from the Lord (James 1:17)

Fear not, for I am with you (Isaiah 41:10)

God is Love (1 John 4:16)

He cares for you (1 Peter 5:7)

I am the Bread of Life (John 6:35)

Jesus said, "let the little children come to Me" (Matt 19:14)

Kind words are like honey, enjoyable and healthful (Prov 16:24)

Love ye one another (John 13:34)

"**M**y sheep hear My voice, and I know them, and they know Me" (John 10:27)

Now is the time to come to Jesus (2 Cor 6:2)

Obey God because you are His children (1 Peter 1:14)

Pray about everything (Phil 4:6)

Quick Lord, answer me, for I have prayed (Psalm 141:1)

Remember your Creator now, while you are young (Eccles 12:1)

Sing a new song to the Lord (Psalm 98:1)

Thank God for Jesus, His gift too wonderful for words (2 Cor 9:15)

· · · · · · · · · · · · · · · ·

<u>U</u>nderneath are God's everlasting arms (Deut 33:27)

<u>V</u>isit the orphans and widows (James 1:27)

<u>W</u>e love because God first loved us (1 John 4:19)

<u>X</u> eXalt His Holy name (Psalm 117)

<u>Y</u>ou must be born again (John 3:7)

"<u>Z</u>acchaeus, you come down, for I'm going to your house today"
   (Luke 19:5)

ESCRITURAS PARA CADA LETRA DE ALFABETO

Todos pecaron y no alcanzaron la Gloria de Dios (Romanos 3:23)

Sé amable el uno con el otro (Ef. 4:32)

Los niños obedecen a tus padres, porque esto es lo correcto (Ef. 6: 1)

No se preocupe ni se preocupe, solo daña (Salmo 37: 8)

Todo don bueno y perfecto viene del Señor (Santiago 1:17)

No temas, porque yo estoy contigo (Isaías 41:10)

Dios es amor (1 Juan 4:16)

Él se preocupa por ti (1 Pedro 5: 7)

Yo soy el pan de vida (Juan 6:35)

Jesús dijo: "que los niños vengan a mí" (Mateo 19:14)

Las palabras amables son como la miel, agradables y saludables (Prov. 16:24)

Amaos los unos a los otros (Juan 13:34)

"Mis ovejas oyen mi voz, y yo las conozco y ellas me conocen" (Juan 10:27)

Ahora es el momento de venir a Jesús (2 Cor 6: 2)

Obedece a Dios porque eres Sus hijos (1 Pedro 1:14)

Ora por todo (Filipenses 4: 6)

Señor rápido, respóndeme, porque he orado (Salmo 141: 1)

Recuerda a tu Creador ahora, mientras eres joven (Eccles 12: 1)

Cante una nueva canción al Señor (Salmo 98: 1)

Gracias a Dios por Jesús, su don demasiado maravilloso para las palabras (2 Cor 9:15)

Debajo están los brazos eternos de Dios (Deut 33:27)

Visita a los huérfanos y viudas (Santiago 1:27)

Amamos porque Dios nos amó primero (1 Juan 4:19)

X eXalt Su Santo nombre (Salmo 117)

Debes nacer de nuevo (Juan 3: 7)

"Zaqueo, baja, porque hoy voy a tu casa" (Lucas 19: 5)

THE MODEL PRAYER MATTHEW 6:9-13

Therefore, you should pray like this:

Our Father in heaven,
Your name be honored as holy.
[10] Your kingdom come.
Your will be done
on earth as it is in heaven.
[11] Give us today our daily bread.
[12] And forgive us our debts,
as we also have forgiven our debtors.
[13] And do not bring us into temptation,
but deliver us from the evil one.
For Yours is the kingdom and the power
and the glory forever. Amen.

La Oración Modelo Mateo 6: 9-13

Por lo tanto, debes orar así:
Nuestro padre en el cielo,
Tu nombre sea honrado como santo.
10 Venga tu reino.

Tu voluntad se hará

en la Tierra como en el cielo.

11 Danos hoy nuestro pan de cada día.

12 Y perdónanos nuestras deudas,

como también hemos perdonado a nuestros deudores.

13 Y no nos dejes caer en la tentación,

pero líbranos del maligno.

Para ti es el reino y el poder

y la gloria por siempre. Amén.

Seven types of prayer:

1. Communion (All day all the time)
2. Supplication (Lifting up your needs)
3. Intercession (On behalf of others)
4. Spiritual Warfare — There are two types: Dealing with yourself (Your mind is the battlefield) & (Repentance and Forgiveness); Dealing with Satan and demons (Putting on the Full Armor) & (Binding & Loosing)
5. Prayers of Agreement (Corporate Prayer)
6. Watch & Pray (Continual State of Awareness as a Watchman on the Wall)
7. Prayers of Thanksgiving (Count your Blessings name them one by one)

Siete tipos de oración

1. Comunión (todo el día todo el tiempo)
2. Súplica (elevando sus necesidades)
3. Intercesión (en nombre de otros)

4. Guerra espiritual: hay dos tipos: tratar contigo mismo (tu mente es el campo de batalla) y (arrepentimiento y perdón); Tratar con Satanás y los demonios (ponerse la armadura completa) y (atar y soltar)

5. Oraciones de acuerdo (oración corporativa)

6. Watch & Pray (Estado continuo de conciencia como vigilante en la pared)

7. Oraciones de Acción de Gracias (Cuenta tus bendiciones, nómbralas una por una)

MEMORY VERSES

Proverbs 9:10

Proverbs 4:23 23

Proverbs 10:11 11

Proverbs 10:4-5 4

Proverbs 3:9-10 9 9

Proverbs 25:21-22 21

Proverbs 3:5

Ephesians 6:2"

Exodus 20:12

Psalm 107:1

Psalm 139:14

Proverbs 3:5-6

Proverbs 13:20

Isaiah 40:28

Jeremiah 29:11

Matthew 28:19-20

Matthew 22:37-39

Luke 6:31

John 3:16

2 Corinthians 9:7

Ephesians 4:32

Philippians 4:6

Philippians 4:13

Colossians 3:20

1 Peter 5:8

1 John 4:19

BOOKS OF THE BIBLE

OLD TESTAMENT		NEW TESTAMENT	
GENESIS	ECCLESIASTES	MATTHEW	JAMES
EXODUS	SONG OF SOLOMON	MARK	1 PETER
LEVITICUS	ISAIAH	LUKE	2 PETER
NUMBERS	JEREMIAH	JOHN	1 JOHN
DEUTERONOMY	LAMENTATIONS	ACTS	2 JOHN
JOSHUA	EZEKIEL	ROMANS	3 JOHN
JUDGES	DANIEL	1 CORINTHIANS	JUDE
RUTH	HOSEA	2 CORINTHIANS	REVELATION
1 SAMUEL	JOEL	GALATIANS	
2 SAMUEL	AMOS	EPHESIANS	
1 KINGS	OBEDIAH	PHILIPPIANS	
2 KINGS	JONAH	COLSSIANS	
1 CHRONICLES	MICAH	1 THESSALONIANS	
EZRA	NAHUN	2 THESSALONIANS	
NEHEMIAH	HABAKKUK	1 TIMOTHY	
ESTER	ZEPHANIAH	2 TIMOTHY	
JOB	HAGGAI	TITUS	
PSALMS	ZECHARIAH	PHILEMON	
PROVERBS	MALACHI	HEBREWS	

LIBROS DE LA BIBLIA

ANTIGUO TESTAMENTO NUEVO TESTAMENTO
GENESIS ECCLESIASTES MATTHEW JAMES
EXODUS CANCIÓN DE SOLOMON MARK 1 PETER
LEVITICUS ISAIAH LUKE 2 PETER
NÚMEROS JEREMÍAS JUAN 1 JUAN
DEUTERONOMÍA LAMENTACIONES ACTOS 2 JUAN
JOSHUA EZEQUIEL ROMANOS 3 JUAN
JUECES DANIEL 1 CORINTHIANS JUDE
RUTH HOSEA 2 REVELACIÓN DE CORINTIOS
1 SAMUEL JOEL GALATAS
2 SAMUEL AMOS EFESIOS
1 REYES OBEDIAS FILIPANAS
2 REYES JONAH COLSSIANS
1 CRÓNICAS MICAH 1 TESALONICENSES
EZRA NAHUN 2 TESALONICENSES
NEHEMIAH HABAKKUK 1 TIMOTEO
ESTER ZEPHANIAH 2 TIMOTEO
TRABAJO HAGGAI TITUS
SALMOS FILAMONO DE ZECARIA
PROVERBIOS HEBREOS DE MALACHI

LET'S CREATE A RAP SONG FOR
THE OLD TESTAMENT BOOKS

Example: Genesis the first book, the book of the beginnings

Creemos una canción de rap para los Libros del Antiguo Testamento
Ejemplo: Génesis el primer libro, el libro de los comienzos

LET'S CREATE A RAP SONG FOR
THE NEW TESTAMENT BOOKS

Example: Matthew, the first book of the New Testament

Creemos una canción de rap para los Libros del Nuevo Testamento
Ejemplo: Mateo, el primer libro del Nuevo Testamento.

QUIZ

1) **The creation of the world is found in the _____.**
   - ⭕ New Testament
   - ⭕ Old Testament

2) **The birth of Jesus is found in the _____.**
   - ⭕ New Testament
   - ⭕ Old Testament

3) **Jesus' baptism is found in the _____.**
   - ⭕ New Testament
   - ⭕ Old Testament

4) **The deliverance of the Children of Israel is found in the _____.**
   - ⭕ New Testament
   - ⭕ Old Testament

5) **The writings of Isaiah are found in the _____.**
   - ⭕ New Testament
   - ⭕ Old Testament

6) **The conversion of Paul is found in the _____.**
   - ○ New Testament
   - ○ Old Testament

7) **The battle of Jericho is found in the _____.**
   - ○ New Testament
   - ○ Old Testament

8) **The story of David & Goliath is found in the _____.**
   - ○ New Testament
   - ○ Old Testament

9) **The story of Daniel in the lion's den is found in the _____.**
   - ○ New Testament
   - ○ Old Testament

EXAMEN

1) La creación del mundo se encuentra en _____.
   Nuevo Testamento
   Viejo Testamento

2) El nacimiento de Jesús se encuentra en el _____.
   Nuevo Testamento
   Viejo Testamento

3) El bautismo de Jesús se encuentra en _____.
   Nuevo Testamento
   Viejo Testamento

4) La liberación de los hijos de Israel se encuentra en el _____.
   Nuevo Testamento
   Viejo Testamento

5) Los escritos de Isaías se encuentran en _____.
   Viejo Testamento
   Viejo Testamento

6) La conversión de Pablo se encuentra en _____.
   Viejo Testamento
   Viejo Testamento

7) La batalla de Jericó se encuentra en el _____.
   Nuevo Testamento
   Viejo Testamento

8) La historia de David y Goliat se encuentra en_____.
   Nuevo Testamento
   Viejo Testamento

9) La historia de Daniel en el foso de los leones se
   encuentra en _____.
   Viejo Testamento
   Viejo Testamento

BOOKS OF THE BIBLE QUIZ

Where is the Scripture Found?

1) **3 John**
   - ⭕ New Testament
   - ⭕ Old Testament

2) **Nehemiah**
   - ⭕ New Testament
   - ⭕ Old Testament

3) **Haggai**
   - ⭕ New Testament
   - ⭕ Old Testament

4) **2 Peter**
   - ⭕ New Testament
   - ⭕ Old Testament

5) **Joshua**
   - ⭕ New Testament
   - ⭕ Old Testament

6) **Jude**
   - ⭕ New Testament
   - Old Testamentt

7) **Ezra**
   - ⭕ New Testament
   - ⭕ Old Testament

8) **Amos**
   - ⭕ New Testament
   - ⭕ Old Testament

9) **Matthew**
   - ⭕ New Testament
   - ⭕ Old Testament

10) **Hosea**
    - ⭕ New Testament
    - ⭕ Old Testament

11) **Luke**
- ○ New Testament
- ○ Old Testament

12) **Acts**
- ○ New Testament
- ○ Old Testament

13) **2 Chronicles**
- ○ New Testament
- ○ Old Testament

14) **1 Thessalonians**
- ○ New Testament
- ○ Old Testament

15) **Jeremiah**
- ○ New Testament
- ○ Old Testament

16) **Obadiah**
- ○ New Testament
- ○ Old Testament

17) **Philippians**
- ○ New Testament
- ○ Old Testament

18) **1 Chronicles**
- ○ New Testament
- ○ Old Testament

19) **Micah**
- ○ New Testament
- ○ Old Testament

20) **Galatians**
- ○ New Testament
- ○ Old Testament

21) **1 Corinthians**
- ○ New Testament
- ○ Old Testament

22) **Isaiah**
- ○ New Testament
- ○ Old Testament

23) **Joel**
- ○ New Testament
- ○ Old Testament

24) **1 Timothy**
- ○ New Testament
- ○ Old Testament

25) **Leviticus**
- ○ New Testament
- ○ Old Testament

26) **2 Kings**
- ○ New Testament
- ○ Old Testament

· · · · · · · · · · · · · · ·

27) **Titus**
- O New Testament
- O Old Testament

28) **Hebrews**
- O New Testament
- O Old Testament

29) **1 Kings**
- O New Testament
- O Old Testament

30) **Ecclesiastes**
- O New Testament
- O Old Testament

31) **1 Peter**
- O New Testament
- O Old Testament

32) **1 John**
- O New Testament
- O Old Testament

33) **Proverbs**
- O New Testament
- O Old Testament

34) **2 John**
- O New Testament
- O Old Testament

35) **Judges**
- O New Testament
- O Old Testament

36) **Psalms**
- O New Testament
- O Old Testament

37) **Jonah**
- O New Testament
- O Old Testament

38) **James**
- O New Testament
- O Old Testament

39) **Genesis**
- O New Testament
- O Old Testament

40) **Song of Solomon**
- O New Testament
- O Old Testament

41) **Philemon**
- O New Testament
- O Old Testament

42) **Revelation**
- O New Testament
- O Old Testament

43) **2 Timothy**
- O New Testament
- O Old Testament

44) **Daniel**
- O New Testament
- O Old Testament

45) **Zechariah**
- O New Testament
- O Old Testament

46) **2 Thessalonians**
- O New Testament
- O Old Testament

47) **2 Corinthians**
- O New Testament
- O Old Testament

48) **Malachi**
- O New Testament
- O Old Testament

49) **Ephesians**
- O New Testament
- O Old Testament

50) **Exodus**
- O New Testament
- O Old Testament

51) **Job**
- O New Testament
- O Old Testament

52) **Colossians**
- O New Testament
- O Old Testament

53) **Ruth**
- O New Testament
- O Old Testament

54) **Esther**
- O New Testament
- O Old Testament

55) **Zephaniah**
- O New Testament
- O Old Testament

56) **Numbers**
- O New Testament
- O Old Testament

57) **Lamentations**
- O New Testament
- O Old Testament

58) **Ezekiel**
- O New Testament
- O Old Testament

59) Habakkuk
○ New Testament
○ Old Testament

60) Romans
○ New Testament
○ Old Testament

61) 1 Samuel
○ New Testament
○ Old Testament

62) Nahum
○ New Testament
○ Old Testament

63) John
○ New Testament
○ Old Testament

64) Deuteronomy
○ New Testament
○ Old Testament

65) 2 Samuel
○ New Testament
○ Old Testament

66) Mark
○ New Testament
○ Old Testament

FILL IN THE BLANK

In the beginning God _____ the heavens and the earth.

The Lord is my _____ I shall not want.

Honor your _____ and _____

Greater is _____ who is in _____ than he that is in the world.

Now abides _____, _____, and _____, the greatest of these is _____.

I waited patiently for the Lord and He inclined his _____.

I can do all _____through _____ who strengthens me.

It is _____ to please God without _____.

He will open up the _____of heaven and pour you out a blessing.

I will _____ the Lord at all times.

Let not your _____ be troubled.

At the name of _____Every _____ must bow.

Confess with your _____ and believe in your _____

COMPLETE EL ESPACIO EN BLANCO

En el principio Dios _____ los cielos y la tierra.

El Señor es mi _____ No querré. Honra
tu _____ y _____ Mayor es
_____ quien está en _____ que el que está en el mundo.
Ahora cumple con _____, _____ y
_____, el mayor de ellos es _____.

Esperé pacientemente al Señor y Él inclinó su _____.

Puedo hacer todo _____ hasta _____ que me
fortalece.

Es _____ agradar a Dios
sin _____.

Él abrirá el _____ del cielo y te derramará una
bendición. _____ al Señor en todo momento. No se
turbe su _____.

A nombre de _____ Cada _____
debe inclinarse. Confiesa con tu _____ y cree
en tu _____

SELECT ONE ANSWER FOR EACH QUESTION ON BOOK OF GENESIS.

1) **Genesis begins with the story of creation. Which is the correct order of creation according to Genesis?**
   - ○ Light; sky; birds and fish; animals and man; earth and plants; heavenly lights;
   - ○ Light; sky; birds and fish; earth and plants; heavenly lights; animals and man
   - ○ Light; sky; earth and plants; heavenly lights; birds and fish; animals and man
   - ○ Light; heavenly lights; sky; birds and fish; earth and plants; animals and man

2) **God created Adam first, then Eve to be his wife and helper. How was Eve, the first woman, created?**
   - ○ God created her from the clay of the ground.
   - ○ God created her from one of Adam's ribs.
   - ○ Adam wished for a helper and God sent Eve into the Garden of Eden.
   - ○ The serpent created her and filled her with evil thoughts.

3) **God placed Adam and Eve in the Garden of Eden and told them they could eat of anything except one forbidden fruit. Which fruit did God tell Adam and Eve they must not eat?**
   - O Fruit from the apple tree.
   - O Fruit from the tree in the middle of the garden.
   - O Fruit from the pomegranate tree
   - O Fermented grapes from the vine.

4) **Of course, they ate the forbidden fruit anyway. What was Eve's excuse when confronted by God?**
   - O "The serpent deceived me, and I ate."
   - O My husband gave me some fruit from the tree, and I ate."
   - O "The devil made me do it."
   - O "The serpent promised me knowledge of good and evil if I ate."

5) **God was angry when He found out Adam and Eve had eaten the forbidden fruit, and He drove them out of the Garden of Eden. How did God make sure they would not return and eat from the tree of life?**
   - O He built a tall wall around the Garden.
   - O He drove Adam and Eve so far away that they could never find the way back.
   - O He placed a curse on the garden so that anyone who entered would surely die.
   - O He placed cherubim and a flaming sword to guard the way.

6) **Adam and Eve had sons Cain and Abel. Each brother gave God an offering from the fruits of his labor. God looked with favor on Abel's offering, but not on Cain's. As a result, Cain became jealous and murdered his brother Abel. What was Cain's occupation?**
   - ○ Farmer
   - ○ Hunter
   - ○ Goat keeper
   - ○ Shepherd

7) **What was Cain's punishment for the murder of Abel?**
   - ○ He was put to death.
   - ○ He was banished to the Land of Canaan.
   - ○ He was banned from his occupation and made a restless wanderer on the earth.
   - ○ He was banned from the Garden of Eden

8) **After many years, the people of earth became corrupt and full of violence. Of all people on earth, only Noah and his family were righteous. So, God said to Noah, "I am going to put an end to all people, for the earth is filled with violence because of them."**

   Noah had three sons. Which one of these was *NOT* one of his sons?
   - ○ Enos
   - ○ Japheth
   - ○ Ham
   - ○ Shem

9) **God decided to flood the whole earth and told Noah to build an ark of wood to hold himself, his wife, his sons and their wives. He was also to take a pair, male and female, of each animal on the ark to save them from the flood and repopulate the earth. How many decks did the ark have?**

   ○ two
   ○ three
   ○ four
   ○ seven

---

10) **Many men settled on a plain in Shinar and said to each other, "Come, let's make bricks and bake them thoroughly and, let us build ourselves a city, with a tower that reaches to the heavens so that we may make a name for ourselves." So, they began constructing the "Tower of Babel."**

   However, God was not pleased with these arrogant men who wanted to build a tower to heaven and be like gods themselves. What did God do to punish them?

   ○ He destroyed the city in a storm of fire and brimstone.
   ○ He confused their language and scattered them over the face of the earth.
   ○ He destroyed the tower with a tremendous bolt of lightning.
   ○ He sent a plague of locusts into the city.

WRITE IN ANSWERS

What is the name of Jesus
mother? _____

Who is God's
son? _____

Who created the heavens and the
earth? _____

Where was Jesus
born? _____

What is FATHER, SON, and HOLY GHOST
CALLED? _____

Once saved always _____

Man ought to always _____

God gave His only begotten _____ so that we might have everlasting life.

God hears and answers _____.

When you win the battle you have _____.

What is the type of love that God has? _____

What is the opposite of sad? _____

NOW FIND THE ANSWERS IN THE
WORD SCRAMBLE GAME & CIRCLE

Y	Y	T	N	I	R	T	M
A	R	A	Y	P	P	A	H
P	G	O	D	Y	R	A	M
A	T	A	T	Y	C	A	O
H	A	P	P	C	H	E	Y
J	E	S	U	S	I	T	P
A	G	A	P	E	E	V	A
S	A	V	E	D	R	T	R
Y	Y	T	N	I	R	T	M
A	R	A	Y	P	P	A	H
P	G	O	D	Y	R	A	M
A	T	A	T	Y	C	A	O
H	A	P	P	C	H	E	Y
J	E	S	U	S	I	T	P
A	G	A	P	E	E	V	A
P	R	A	Y	E	R	T	R

ESCRIBE EN RESPUESTAS

¿Cómo se llama la madre de
Jesús? _____

¿Quién es el hijo de
Dios? _____

¿Quién creó los cielos y la
tierra? _____

¿Dónde nació
Jesús? _____

¿Qué se llama PADRE, HIJO y SANTO
FANTASMA? _____

Una vez guardado siempre _____

El hombre siempre debe _____

Dios dio a su unigénito _____ para que tengamos vida
eterna.

Dios escucha y responde _____.

· · · · · · · · · · · · · · · ·

Cuando ganas la batalla tienes _____.

¿Cuál es el tipo de amor que Dios tiene? _____

¿Qué es lo contrario de triste? _____

Angels are helpers of God. True or False. (circle answer)

Find a scripture to back up your answer and write it below. Write the scripture and verse.

Los ángeles son ayudantes de Dios. Verdadero o falso. (circule la respuesta)

Encuentre una escritura para respaldar su respuesta y escríbala a continuación. Escribe la escritura y el verso.

_____
_____
_____
_____
_____
_____
_____
_____
_____
_____
_____
_____
_____

· · · · · · · · · · · · · ·

THE BIBLE IS THE WORD OF GOD. FIND A SCRIPTURE THAT LETS US KNOW THIS IS TRUE.

Write it in the space below. Give the scripture reference.

La Biblia es la Palabra de Dios. Encuentre una escritura que nos permita saber que esto es cierto.

Escríbelo en el espacio de abajo. Da la referencia de las Escrituras.

_____

_____

_____

_____

_____

_____

_____

_____

_____

_____

_____

_____

_____

THE CROSS – WHERE JESUS DIED

Who crucified Jesus? _____

Had He done anything to deserve to
die? _____

Draw a picture of the Cross in the space below.

La cruz-donde murió Jesús

¿Quién crucificó a Jesús? _____

¿Había hecho algo para merecer
morir? _____

Haz un dibujo de la Cruz en el espacio de abajo.

FAITH – IT IS IMPOSSIBLE TO
PLEASE GOD WITHOUT FAITH

UNSCRAMBLE THE WORDS TO EXPLAIN WHY
(may not need all the letters)

TSUM EVBLIVE ____ ____ ____ ____ ____ ____ ____

Dbbse crere ____ ____ ____ ____ ____ ____ ____

SDSEJUEID

____ ____ ____ ____ ____ ____ ____ ____ ____

Jusus ourim____ ____ ____ ____ ____ ____ ____

EROSC ____ ____ ____ ____

sora ____ ____ ____ ____

RELAINGVLFEST IE ____ ____ ____ ____ ____ ____ ____

____ ____ ____ ____

Vida Eterna ____ _____ ____ _____ ____ ____ ____ ____ ____

____ _____

EHT NSINRES SAIORV__ ____ ____ _____ _____ _____ ____

Saladorv a los rdesuciaost

____ ____ ____ _____ _____ _____ ____

Man looks on outward appearances. What does God look upon?
Draw a picture of it for your answer.

El hombre mira las apariencias externas. ¿Qué mira Dios?
Haz un dibujo para tu respuesta

Can't figure out answer unscrample the word TRAEH
No puedo entender la respuesta descifrar la palabra CORAZÓN

What is a servant?
¿Qué es un sirviente?

What role does a servant have for Jesus?
¿Qué papel tiene un siervo para Jesús?

What is the difference in a slave and a servant?
¿Cuál es la diferencia en un esclavo y un sirviente?

What are some of the names of God?
¿Cuáles son algunos de los nombres de Dios?

UNSCRAMBLE WORDS FOR THE ANSWER

OVHAJEH ___ ____ ____ ____ ____ ____ ____GOD

JRIEH ____ ____ ____ ____ ____PROVIDER

ADDAIHS___ ____ ____ ____ ____ ____GOD ALMIGHTY

YAEHWE ____ ___ ____ ____ ____ ____ I AM THAT I AM

ALSOMH ____ ____ ____ ____ ____ ____ PEACE

PRAPHA ___ ____ ____ ___ ____ ____ HEALER

0IELR ____ ____ ____ ____ ____ ALL SEEING

MIHLOE ____ ____ ____ ____ ____ GOD OF AUTHORITY
GOD OF AUTHORITY

LUEMANIM____ ____ ____ ____ ____ ____ ____ ____ ____
GOD WITH US

AONAID ___ ____ ____ ____ ____ ____ MASTER

NOLYE ___ ____ ____ ____ ____ SUPREME

DRAW A LINE TO THE MEANING OF WORD

COMPASSION

GOD'S LOVE

GRACE

NOT EATING

PRAYING

SING

HAPPINESS

FORGIVENESS

BROTHERS & SISTERS

SHOW KINDNESS

SON OF GOD

COMMIT WRONGS

PEACE

PRAISE

UNMERITED LOVE

BENDED KNEES

MERCY

FAMILY

NO LONGER HOLD
RESPONSIBLE

SIN

LOVE

JESUS

HARMONY WITH VOICE

JOY

FASTING

UNMERITED FAVOR

WHO ARE THE HELPERS OF GOD?

DRAW ONE

¿QUIÉNES SON LOS AYUDANTES DE DIOS?

_____ _____ _____ _____ _____ _____

DIBUJA UNO

Answer (Angels)

Respuesta (ángeles)

WHERE DO WE GO TO WORSHIP?

____ ____ ____ ____ ____ ____

DRAW ONE

¿A DÓNDE VAMOS A ADORAR? ____ ____
____ ____ ____ ____ DIBUJA UNO

Answer: CHURCH

Respuesta: IGLESIA

CREATE YOUR OWN WORD GAME

CREA TU PROPIO JUEGO DE PALABRAS

1. _____

2. _____

3. _____

4. _____

5. _____

6. _____

7. _____

8. _____

9. _____

CUT OUTS

CREATE A PICTURE

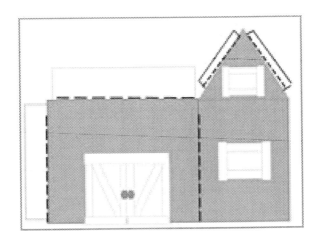

What relationship was Jesus to John the
Baptist? _____

¿Qué relación tenía Jesús con Juan el
Bautista? _____

Who was born first Jesus or John the
Baptist? _____

¿Quién nació primero Jesús o Juan el
Bautista? _____

Who was Jesus'
mother? _____

¿Quién era la madre de
Jesús? _____

Who was John the Baptist
mother? _____

¿Quién era la madre de John the
Babtist? _____

Where was Jesus
born? _____

¿Dónde nació
Jesús?_____

What town was Jesus
born in?_____

¿En qué pueblo nació
Jesús? _____

CREATE YOUR OWN PUZZLE

Use Biblical words or Bible Verses

UNSCRAMBLE WORDS

L R N F E O D U W _____

L E B I R V E E   _____

S E S U J   _____

E F C R I A I C S _____

L S U O   _____

C R E N P I   _____

C E A P E   _____

J E Y R N O U   _____

R A C P E H R E _____

Y N I R I T T   _____

F L J O U Y   _____

NOW CREATE YOUR OWN SCRAMBLE WORD GAME AND HAVE
FRIEND SOLVE

1._____   _____

2._____   _____

3._____   _____

4._____   _____

5._____   _____

6._____   _____

7._____   _____

8._____   _____

9._____   _____

10._____   _____

TRACE YOUR HAND FRONTWARDS AND BACKWARDS
THEN DRAW IT ON NEXT SHEET.

RASTREA TU MANO DELANTERO Y HACIA ATRÁS
LUEGO DIBUJA EN LA PRÓXIMA HOJA.

DRAW YOUR HAND

WRITE YOUR NAME IN SIGN
DRAW HAND SIGN AS BEST AS YOU CAN. SEE CHART

DIBUJA TU MANO
ESCRIBE TU NOMBRE AL FIRMAR
DIBUJA LA FIRMA A MANO LO MEJOR
QUE PUEDAS. VE LA TABLA

_____ _____ _____ _____ _____

_____ _____ _____ _____ _____

_____ _____ _____ _____ _____

_____ _____ _____ _____ _____

_____ _____ _____ _____ _____

DRAW THE SIGN LANGUAGE HAND SIGN FOR J E S U S

Draw the Sign Language Hand Sign for <u>GOD</u>

CHOOSE A BIBLICAL NAME AND DRAW THE HAND SIGN

WRITE THE NAME_____

DRAW HAND SIGNS IN SPACE BELOW

ELIGE UN NOMBRE BÍBLICO Y SORTEA EL SIGNO DE MANO

ESCRIBE EL NOMBRE_____

SORTEA LOS SIGNOS DE MANO EN EL ESPACIO ABAJO

ARE THESE SCRIPTURE/IN THE BIBLE? IF SO WHERE

¿ESTAS ESCRITURAS / EN LA BIBLIA? SI ES ASÍ, DONDE

HONOR YOUR FATHER AND MOTHER
Honra a tu madre y a tu padre

OBEDIENCE IS BETTER THAN SACRIFICE
LA OBEDIENCIA ES MEJOR QUE EL SACRIFICIO

WHEN PRAISES GO UP BLESSINGS COME DOWN
Cuando las alabanzas suben, las bendiciones bajan

IT IS BETTER TO GIVE THAN TO RECEIVE
ES MEJOR DAR QUE RECIBIR

GOD DOES NOT GIVE US A SPIRIT OF FEAR
DIOS NO NOS DA UN ESPÍRITU DE TEMOR

I SHALL COME FORTH LIKE PURE GOLD
VENDRÉ COMO EL ORO PURO

GOD IS LOVE
DIOS ES AMOR

IT IS IMPOSSIBLE TO PLEASE GOD WITHOUT FAITH
ES IMPOSIBLE POR FAVOR DIOS SIN FE

NOW ABIDES FAITH, HOPE, LOVE, THESE THREE, BUT THE
    GREATEST OF THESE IS LOVE
AHORA ABANDONE FE, ESPERANZA, AMOR, ESTOS TRES,
    PERO LO MAYOR DE ESTO ES AMOR

I CAN DO ALL THINGS THROUGH CHRIST WHO STRENGTHENS
    ME
PUEDO HACER TODAS LAS COSAS A TRAVÉS DE CRISTO QUE
    ME FORTALECE

GREATER IS HE THAT IS WITHIN ME THAN he THAT IS IN THE
    WORLD
MAYOR ES EL QUE ESTÁ DENTRO DE MÍ QUE EL QUE ESTÁ EN
    EL MUNDO

NO GREATER LOVE THAN A MAN LAY DOWN HIS LIFE FOR A
    FRIEND
NO HAY MAYOR AMOR QUE UN HOMBRE DICE SU VIDA PARA
    UN AMIGO

NO WEAPON FORMED AGAINST ME SHALL PROSPER
NINGUNA ARMA FORJADA CONTRA MÍ PROSPERARÁ

MAN OUGHT TO ALWAYS PRAY
EL HOMBRE DEBE ORAR SIEMPRE

LOVE THY NEIGHBOR AS THYSELF
AMA A TU VECINO COMO A TI MISMO

Answers to Names of God Scramble

Jehovah

Jireh

Shaddai

Shalom

Rappha

Elroi

Elohim

Emanuel

Adonai

Elyon

Answers to Word Scramble

Wonderful

Believer

Jesus

Sacrifice

Soul

Prince

Peace

Journey

Preacher

Trinity

Joyful

Answer to Faith Scramble

Must believe

Jesus Died

Rose

Save the sinner

Everlasting life

Answer to Activity and (find the word)

Mary

Jesus

God

Bethlehem

Trinity

Saved

Pray

Son

Prayers

Victory

Acape

Happy

Answers to fill in the Blank

Created

Shepherd

Mother, father

He, Me

Faith, hope, love love

Ear

Things, Christ

Impossible, faith

Windows

Bless

heart

Jesus, knee

Mouth, heart

Answers to Quiz on Book of Genesis

Light; sky; earth and plants; heavenly lights; birds and fish; animals and man

---

God created her from one of Adam's ribs.

Fruit from the tree in the middle of the garden.

"The serpent deceived me, and I ate."

He placed cherubim and a flaming sword to guard the way.

Farmer

He was banned from his occupation and made a restless wanderer on the earth.

Enos

---

three

He confused their language and scattered them over the face of the earth.

ONE WAY ON HOW TO STUDY THE BIBLE

Choose a book. In this method you will study an entire book of the Bible, one at time. If you've never done this before, start with a small book, preferably from the New Testament. The book of James, Titus, 1 Peter, or 1 John are all good choices for first-timers. Plan to spend 3-4 weeks studying the book you have chosen. Before you start each study session, begin by praying and asking God to open your spiritual understanding. The Bible says in 2 Timothy 3:16, *"All Scripture is inspired by God and profitable for teaching, reproof/ rebuking, for correction and training in righteousness."* (NASB) So, as you pray, realize that the words you are studying are inspired by God. Psalm 119:130 tells us, *"The unfolding of His words give light; it gives understanding to the simple."*

Next you'll spend some time, perhaps several days, reading through the entire book. Do this more than once. Think about who is speaking and who is being spoken to. As you read, look for themes that may be woven into the chapters. Sometimes you'll detect a general message in the book. For example, in the book of James, an obvious theme is "Persevering or continuing to work through Trials." Take notes on the ideas that jump out at you.

Look also for "life application principles." An example of a life application principle in the book of James is: "Make sure my faith is more than just a statement-it should result in action." It's a good practice to try and pull out these themes and applications on your own as you meditate, even before you begin using other study tools. This gives an opportunity for God's Word to speak personally to you.

Now let's see what it looks like under a microscope, as we begin breaking down the text. Using a Bible dictionary, look up the meaning of the word **living** in the original language. It is the Greek word **'Zaõ'** meaning, *"not only living, but causing to live, quickening."* You start to see a deeper meaning: *"God's Word causes life to come about; it quickens."* Because God's Word is alive, you can study the same passage several times and continue to discover new, relevant applications throughout your walk of faith.

As you continue to do this type of verse by verse study, there's no limit to the wealth of understanding and growth that will come from your time spent in God's Word. For this portion of your study, you will want to consider choosing the right tools to aid you in your learning, such as a commentary, lexicon or Bible dictionary. A Bible study guide or perhaps a study Bible will also help you dig deeper. Check out the NASB as suggested by Pastor R A Vernon on great Bibles for Bible study. There are also many useful on-line Bible study resources available, if you have access to a computer for your study time.

Don't just study God's Word for the sake of studying. Be sure to put the Word into practice in your life/life application. Jesus said in Luke 11:28, *"But even more blessed are all who hear the word of God and put it into practice."* Once you've finished the first book, choose another one and follow the same steps. You may want to spend much more time digging into the Old Testament and some of the longer books of the Bible.

COMO ESTUDIAR LA BIBLIA

Escoge un libro. En este método estudiarás un libro completo de la Biblia, uno a la vez. Si nunca ha hecho esto antes, comience con un libro pequeño, preferiblemente del Nuevo Testamento. El libro de Santiago, Tito, 1 Pedro o 1 Juan son buenas opciones para los novatos. Planee pasar 3-4 semanas estudiando el libro que ha elegido. Antes de comenzar cada sesión de estudio, comience orando y pidiéndole a Dios que abra su comprensión espiritual. La Biblia dice en 2 Timoteo 3:16: "Toda la Escritura está inspirada por Dios y es provechosa para la enseñanza, la represión / el reproche, la corrección y el entrenamiento en la justicia". (NASB) Entonces, mientras oras, date cuenta de que las palabras que estás estudiando están inspiradas por Dios. El Salmo 119: 130 nos dice: "El desarrollo de sus palabras da luz; da entendimiento a los simples".

A continuación, pasará algún tiempo, tal vez varios días, leyendo todo el libro. Haz esto más de una vez. Piensa en quién habla y con quién se habla. Mientras lees, busca temas que puedan estar entretejidos en los capítulos. A veces detectará un mensaje general en el libro. Por ejemplo, en el libro de James, un tema obvio es "Perseverar o continuar trabajando en los ensayos". Toma notas sobre las ideas que te llaman la atención

Busque también "principios de aplicación de la vida". Un ejemplo de un principio de aplicación de la vida en el libro de James es: "Asegúrate de que mi fe sea más que una simple declaración: debe dar lugar a una acción". Es una buena práctica intentar extraer estos temas y aplicaciones por su cuenta mientras medita, incluso antes de comenzar a usar otras herramientas de estudio. Esto le da la oportunidad a la Palabra de Dios de hablarle personalmente.

Ahora veamos cómo se ve bajo un microscopio, a medida que comenzamos a desglosar el texto. Usando un diccionario bíblico, busque el significado de la palabra que vive en el idioma original. Es la palabra griega 'Zaõ' que significa "no solo vivir, sino hacer que viva, se acelere". Empiezas a ver un significado más profundo: "La Palabra de Dios hace que la vida surja; se acelera". Debido a que la Palabra de Dios está viva, puede estudiar el mismo pasaje varias veces y continuar descubriendo aplicaciones nuevas y relevantes a lo largo de su camino de fe.

A medida que continúe haciendo este tipo de estudio verso por verso, no hay límite para la riqueza de comprensión y crecimiento que resultará de su tiempo dedicado a la Palabra de Dios. Para esta parte de tu estudio, deberás considerar elegir las herramientas adecuadas para ayudarte en tu aprendizaje, como un comentario, un léxico o un diccionario bíblico. Una guía de estudio bíblico o tal vez una Biblia de estudio también lo ayudará a profundizar. Echa un vistazo a la NASB según lo sugerido por el Pastor R A Vernon sobre excelentes Biblias para el estudio de la Biblia. También hay muchos recursos útiles de estudio bíblico en línea disponibles, si tiene acceso a una computadora para su tiempo de estudio.

· · · · · · · · · · · · · ·

No solo estudies la Palabra de Dios por el simple hecho de estudiar. Asegúrese de poner en práctica la Palabra en su aplicación de vida / vida. Jesús dijo en Lucas 11:28: "Pero aún más bendecidos son todos los que escuchan la palabra de Dios y la ponen en práctica". Una vez que haya terminado el primer libro, elija otro y siga los mismos pasos. Es posible que desee pasar mucho más tiempo investigando el Antiguo Testamento y algunos de los libros más largos de la Biblia.

TIPS ON HOW TO STUDY THE BIBLE

Five Principles of Bible study
- Ask the right questions.
- Write down what you observe and discover.
- Apply your discovery to your life and thoughts.
- Study the Bible systematically.
- Strive to exhaust the passage you are studying.

Bible Study Tools in Order of Importance
- Translation of the Bible
- Concordance
- Dictionary
- Bible Dictionary
- Commentary

Methodical Bible study
- Pray for the Holy Spirit's guidance and insight.
- Make observations by asking questions.
- Seek answers from the scripture and then tools in order of importance.
- Apply the scripture to your life.

Questions to Ask When Studying the Bible

- What is the historical setting?
- What is the literary form?
- What are the key words?
- What important grammatical structure do I observe?
- What is the tense of the verbs?
- Is there something contrasted?
- Is there a paradox?
- Is the passage dependant on a preceding passage?
- Ask six questions: What? Who? Where? When? Why? and How?

Application of a Bible Passage

- Is there a promise to claim?
- Is there a command to obey?
- Is there a sin to confess?
- Is there a teaching to absorb?

CONSEJOS SOBRE CÓMO ESTUDIAR LA BIBLIA

Cinco principios del estudio bíblico
- Haga las preguntas correctas.
- Escriba lo que observa y descubre.
- Aplique su descubrimiento a su vida y pensamientos.
- Estudie la Biblia sistemáticamente.
- Esfuércese por agotar el pasaje que está estudiando.

Herramientas de estudio bíblico en orden de importancia
- Traducción de la Biblia
- concordancia
- Diccionario
- Diccionario de la Biblia
- Comentario

Estudio metódico de la Biblia
- Ore por la guía y perspicacia del Espíritu Santo.
- Hacer observaciones haciendo preguntas.
- Busque respuestas de las Escrituras y luego herramientas en orden de importancia.
- Aplica la escritura a tu vida.

Preguntas para hacer al estudiar la Biblia
- ¿Cuál es el escenario histórico?
- ¿Cuál es la forma literaria?
- ¿Cuáles son las palabras clave?
- ¿Qué estructura gramatical importante observo?
- ¿Cuál es el tiempo de los verbos?
- ¿Hay algo contrastado?
- ¿Hay una paradoja?
- ¿El pasaje depende de un pasaje anterior?
- Haga seis preguntas: ¿Qué? ¿Quien? ¿Dónde? ¿Cuando? ¿Por qué? ¿y cómo?

Aplicación de un pasaje bíblico
- ¿Hay alguna promesa que reclamar?
- ¿Hay una orden de obedecer?
- ¿Hay un pecado que confesar?
- ¿Hay una enseñanza para absorber?

ONLINE RESOURCES FOR STUDYING THE BIBLE

Studylight.org

Bibegateway.com

Into Thy Word Ministries-http://70030.netministry.com/pages.asp?pageid=53515

BIBLE SEARCH LINKS.com

Bible Gateway

Blue Letter Bible

WebBible Online

Online Bible choose version

Interlinear Study Bible

Olive Tree Bible Search Engine

Scholarly Technology Group

All in One Biblical Research Search

DICTIONARIES & ENCYCLOPEDIAS

Condensed Biblical Cyclopedia

Jesus of Nazareth Condensed Cyclopedia

Easton's Bible Dictionary

Easton's Bible Dictionary (2)

. . . .

Baker's Evangelical Dictionary
of Biblical Theology
Hitchcock's Bible Names
Jack Van Impe's Dictionary
of Prophecy Terms
King James Dictionary
Smith's Bible Dictionary
Dictionary of Bible Words as Symbols
Bible Defintions

CONCORDANCES

Strong's Exhaustive Concordance
Nave's Topical Bible
Torrey's Topical Textbook
God's Yellow Pages

RECURSOS EN LÍNEA PARA ESTUDIAR LA BIBLIA.

Studylight.org

Bibegateway.com

En tus ministerios de Word-http://70030.netministry.com/pages.asp?pageid=53515

BIBLIA BÚSQUEDA ENLACES.com

Bible Gateway

Blue Letter Bible

WebBible en línea

Biblia en línea elegir versión

Biblia de estudio interlineal

Buscador de la Biblia del Olivo

Grupo de tecnología académica

Búsqueda de investigación bíblica todo en uno

DICCIONARIOS Y ENCICLOPEDIAS

Cyclopedia Bíblica Condensada

Jesús de Nazaret Cyclopedia Condensada

Diccionario de la Biblia de Easton

Diccionario Bíblico de Easton (2)

Diccionario evangélico de Baker

de teología bíblica

Nombres bíblicos de Hitchcock

Diccionario de Jack Van Impe

de los términos de profecía

Diccionario King James

Diccionario de la Biblia de Smith

Diccionario de palabras de la Biblia como símbolos

Definiciones bíblicas

Concordancias

Concordancia exhaustiva de Strong

Biblia tópica de la nave

Libro de texto de actualidad de Torrey

Páginas amarillas de Dios

MIRACLES AND BLESSINGS

Bible

Angel

By Glenda Louse Smith 2014

Dr. Glenda Smith is married to Darryl Smith, Sr. She is the proud mother of five children, with birthing 2 daughters. She has many adopted children and is loved by all. Dr. Glenda Smith's motto is "I can do all things through Christ who strengthens me." Also, "If I can just be a Blessing to others, my living will not be in vain."

Dr. Glenda Smith is an ordained minister. She was an Associate Minister at Christ Missionary Baptist Church in Memphis, TN under the leadership of Dr. Gina M Stewart where she served more than fifteen years. She currently relocated to Cleveland, Ohio where she serves at The Word Church under the leadership of Dr. R. A. Vernon and works with the Children's Ministry.

Dr. Glenda Smith has an Honorary Doctorate of Divinity from St. Luke Evangelical Bible College and has studied for her Doctorate in Business Administration from Argosy University. She is a graduate from Memphis Theological Seminary with a Masters in Theology. She is a graduate of Central Michigan University with a Master of Science Human Resources. She has a Bachelor of Science in Business Administration from Belhaven College. She graduated from The Tennessee School of Religion with a Bachelor of Arts in Theological Studies. She has attended Cleveland State University.

Dr. Glenda Smith served as a Congressional Specialist to a U. S. Congressman for over six years. She served as the Director of Human Resources for a Non-Profit Organization for four years. Dr. Smith served on the Board of Directors for Drapers' Ministries and Olanda Drapers' Associates and Ruth's Global Outreach Services. She is the author of the Book "Righteous Never Forsaken, Never Beggin' For Bread. She played the role of the preacher in the documentary and movie "The Legend of Little Horse." She was the Co-Host of the

Cable Talk Show "Women of Concern for State of Tennessee" for ten years. She was named an uncommon Hero by Pax Television. She worked a Battle Ground State for President Barak Obama.

Dr. Glenda Smith is married to Darryl Smith, Sr. She is the proud mother of five children, with birthing 2 daughters, a grand mother of 8 and recently a great grand mother. She has many adopted children and is loved by all. Dr. Glenda Smith's motto is "I can do all things through Christ who strengthens me." Also, "If I can just be a Blessing to others, my living will not be in vain."

Dr. Glenda Smith

Printed in the United States
By Bookmasters